ABANDONED RUINS OF
EASTERN PENNSYLVANIA
REMNANTS LOST IN TIME

KATHLEEN BUTLER

AMERICA
THROUGH TIME®
ADDING COLOR TO AMERICAN HISTORY

America Through Time is an imprint of Fonthill Media LLC
www.through-time.com
office@through-time.com

Published by Arcadia Publishing by arrangement with Fonthill Media LLC
For all general information, please contact Arcadia Publishing:
Telephone: 843-853-2070
Fax: 843-853-0044
E-mail: sales@arcadiapublishing.com
For customer service and orders:
Toll-Free 1-888-313-2665

www.arcadiapublishing.com

First published 2020

Copyright © Kathleen Butler 2020

ISBN 978-1-63499-240-4

Typeset in Trade Gothic 10pt on 15pt
Printed and bound in England

CONTENTS

Acknowledgments   **5**

Introduction   **6**

1   Colonial Springs Bottling Plant   **7**

2   Concrete City   **13**

3   Devil's Hole and Fieldstone Farm Preserve Ruins   **18**

4   Mocanaqua Coal Mining Ruins   **25**

5   Abandoned Italian Water Garden   **32**

6   Bear Valley Ghost Town   **36**

7   Lausanne Ghost Town   **40**

8   Thomas Iron Mills Ruins   **46**

9   Poquessing Creek Ruins   **52**

10   Ridley Creek State Park Ruins   **57**

11   Rolling Hill Park Ruins   **62**

12   Monocacy Hill Quarry Ruins   **69**

13   DelHaas Woods Ruins   **74**

14   Marsh Creek Ruins   **79**

15   Wissahickon Valley Ruins   **83**

16   Abandoned and in Ruin   **88**

Bibliography   **95**

ACKNOWLEDGMENTS

None of this would be possible if it weren't for my husband and children. Thank you, Robert, Daniel and Alexandrea, for going on these exploring trips with me.

To my mother, Eileen, and my brother, Frank: thank you for your words of encouragement. I wouldn't be so adventurous if not for you both, and my other brother, Rich—may he rest in peace.

Finally, to the rest of my family and friends for giving me that extra boost of support: thank you!

INTRODUCTION

Histori is disappearing right before our eyes—history that is not taught in schools. We are living in an era where the need for expanding land development is at an all-time high, but some land is not worth developing on, while other land should no longer be touched. In this book, we set out to find ruins in Eastern Pennsylvania that were abandoned for various reasons—such as poor judgement, over industrialization, forces of nature, and more—and learn their history before they are gone forever.

Disclaimer

Take pictures and/or video, but be respectful so others can enjoy and see the natural decay of these abandoned ruins.

Most of these ruins are in the forests of Pennsylvania. It is best to be cautious of your surroundings with wildlife. Snakes tend to hide in crevices and near rocks. Poison ivy and poison oak can also cover these ruins. Explore your world, but know your surroundings and respect nature.

Heed any warnings of private property.

1

COLONIAL SPRINGS BOTTLING PLANT

L ocated in Valley Forge National Historic Park are the ruins of a bottling plant that is located along Horseshoe Trail (yellow blazed path) on Mount Misery in Valley Forge, Pennsylvania. This plant harnessed the pristine water the mountain produced, filtered from the unique geological system on top.

Built in the 1800s, the bottling plant was owned by a Civil War hero named General Benjamin Franklin Fisher. He granted leases for the purchase of the water from the mountain spring that the plant produced. It is unknown exactly when the leases were sold for commercial use, but it was believed to have started in 1908.

The source of the tapped water was the special stone grade of the geological area on top of the mountain more than 600 feet above the bottling plant. The water that was tapped was said to have been pure and clean. During that time, Schuylkill River was extremely polluted, and the bottling plant provided a clean, natural source of drinking water to the surrounding community. The companies that tapped the water stored the product in sterilized, sealed glass bottles.

When Benjamin Franklin Fisher passed away in 1915, the property was sold to Charles Hires, the founder of Hires Root Beer. It is not known if Charles Hires produced the root beer from this bottling plant.

Ultimately, the property was purchased by Valley Forge State Park in the 1930s. Shortly after the purchase, the park took down most of the house that Benjamin Franklin Fisher lived in, just down the path from the bottling plant. Still visible today, small portions of a wall made of stone and concrete remain along the hillside of Mount Misery.

TODAY

The bottling plant ruin still has all four walls intact but no roof. It has recently been reinforced with concrete patchwork on the walls and lumber supports were put in place around the window and door frames to help preserve the remains of the ruin. Much of the original stonework is still visible.

There is a tunnel-like access area inside the bottling plant ruin towards the right corner of the building, but it doesn't go very far. The water from the mountain only trickles and the walls are lined with insects. This is where the water would have been tapped. There is also an area where it seems the collected water was organized for transport.

The bottling plant viewed from the lower part of the trail.

The remains of General Benjamin Franklin Fisher's house.

The bottling plant viewed from the upper part of the trail.

A view inside the bottling plant.

A view of the tunnel-like access area.

Above left: Looking inside the tunnel.

Above right: Inside the tunnel, the wall is lined with insects. Note that it doesn't go very far.

Above left: This could have been a supplemental water tap. It is located in the ruin.

Above right: Along the trail to the ruins remains a fireplace. There are no remnants of any other structures in the immediate area.

2

CONCRETE CITY

Located in Nanticoke, Concrete City was built for the Delaware, Lackawanna and Western Railroad's (DL&W Railroad) railroad and coal mining management in 1911.

There are twenty buildings formed in a rectangle. Outhouses, also made of concrete, were built behind each duplex. In the center of this new community was a courtyard, and it had a playground and a pool, but the pool was filled in when, tragically, a young boy drowned in 1914. The buildings are entirely made of poured concrete, a new and innovative type of architecture for that time.

Only high-level employees of the company were given the option to live in these buildings. The buildings were duplexes—a two-family home that families could live in side-by-side, consisting of seven rooms each.

The mining company thought they were giving only the best to their valued employees, but issues started to arise, and the tenants started to complain. Condensation was seeping through the walls and paint began to peel. Something as easy as keeping clothes from the closet dry became an everyday battle. Wives would often need to iron their husband's clothes before work only to get them dry.

The ultimate demise of Concrete City came when the necessary installation of a sewer system emerged. It was an expensive project that the owners did not want to pay for. In 1924, Concrete City was abandoned.

Many attempts were made to demolish the buildings with dynamite, but the structures seemed almost impervious. Any and all future attempts to bring the buildings down were simply disregarded, as it was deemed too expensive.

TODAY

All twenty buildings still stand. Fireman and policeman use these buildings to train. Sometimes, even paintball players will get a few games in while running and dodging through the buildings.

A few of the buildings have significant damage and caution is advised to those that want to explore this abandoned community. Large concrete fragments hang off the side, only being held on by a piece of metal. One of the buildings seems to be sinking because it is not level, but after 100 years, the sinking process is slow.

Above: Looking at the building in Concrete City, notice how the one window appears to be heavily damaged.

Below: Even the roofs were made of concrete and most are still intact.

A hole in the second-level floor. This could have been from when they tried to destroy the building with dynamite.

Above right: Looking from one building to another on the second floor. Notice the damage to these window frames.

3

DEVIL'S HOLE AND FIELDSTONE FARM PRESERVE RUINS

The Devil's Hole ruins are located deep in the woods on the 4,600+ acres of Pennsylvania State Game Lands #221, and it is rumored they were part of a speakeasy during the Prohibition era in the 1920s, but a reliable source indicates the house was built by a wealthy merchant from New York City who was traveling through the area. He had later built a mansion for his daughter about a quarter-mile away, which is now a part of Fieldstone Farm Preserve. It is believed to have been built in the 1920s or 1930s, perhaps by the same stone mason that built the Devil's Hole ruin.

Devil's Hole ruins were believed to have been a private hunting cabin for the wealthy merchant who, when passing through town one day, fell in love with the scenic beauty the land offered. The land is surrounded by mountains, valleys and pine trees, and it is dense with mountain laurel.

Some people even speculate that it was a ski resort at one time known as the Seven Pines Lodge. Flywheels can still be spotted in trees and there are thick cable lines being devoured by growing trees. These indications of a puzzled past could be hints of speakeasy equipment used to haul bottles of liquor up and down the slope, but one can only speculate their actual purpose.

The name "Devil's Hole" was derived from a legend indicating that a lake once existed in this area. It was said that the lake was bottomless. Anyone who swam in the lake was an unfortunate soul that sank straight to hell. The lake was said to have dissipated with the flood of 1955.

NEIGHBORING STATE GAME LANDS #221

The Fieldstone Farm Preserve mansion sits on 57 acres of land that is privately owned, but managed by Pocono Heritage Land Trust as open space to protect the diversity of the natural lands.

The ruins are located on a hillside, and just below the mansion ruins are two manmade freshwater ponds with what appears to have been a small pump house next to them. The water flows naturally down the hillside and is vital to Tank Creek. The water is still known for its high quality.

The mansion caught fire in the 1960s, and later the barn and chicken house nearby met the same fate.

TODAY

Two very large multi-level chimneys and portions of the foundation, along with other remnants, can still be seen today at the Devil's Hole ruins.

The remains of the Fieldstone Farm Preserve mansion are mostly stone. It is apparent from the singed stonework that this structure caught fire.

A view of Devil's Hole ruins from the trail.

One of two of the multi-level fireplaces. The lower level with mantel would have been for the basement while the next level up would have been for a main floor.

Peering from inside the ruins at Devil's Hole looking out into the forest.

The furnace remains as a part of the Devil's Hole ruins today. Notice the cinder blocks at the upper level of the ruin.

Above left: A frame from a piano or organ inside Devil's Hole ruins.

Above right: A tree growing around a cable near Devil's Hole ruins.

Fieldstone farmhouse as seen from the trail.

A view of Fieldstone farmhouse from what was the front entrance. Notice the burned portions.

Above left: Stairs on the side of Fieldstone farmhouse. Moss and ferns are growing on this portion.

Above right: The back of Fieldstone farmhouse.

Peering inside Fieldstone farmhouse. Nature is taking over.

This could have been a pump house, spring house or storage. It is located near the manmade ponds.

4

MOCANAQUA COAL MINING RUINS

With rich deposits of anthracite coal, the town of Mocanaqua was established by the West End Coal Company in 1882. Coal mining in the area began before the town was established in the 1850s. A coal mining accident first struck in 1885 when a fan that supplied air into the mine for the boilers failed the night before. Gas began building up inside the mine where 150 men were working the very next morning on August 11. The fire boss noticed the gas building up and started giving the alarm. At this point, the miners dropped their load and started making their way out. Accounts from the surviving miners said that as they were trying to get out of the mining tunnels, they noticed hordes of rats also trying to vacate the mine ahead of them. Rats sometimes occupied mining tunnels. This was taken as a good sign to the miners who worked in them. If there were any gas leaks, the rats would start to vacate.

Once the news reached town, family members and doctors made their way to the mine to assist or to see if their loved one was okay. Miners were being pulled out of the mine in makeshift stretchers and most recovered. Gas continued to build up in the mine and efforts to rescue the remaining men ceased later that afternoon. Overall, about twenty men perished in the accident. Rescuers were not able to recover all the bodies.

In October of 1931, tragedy struck again when a mine explosion happened in the same area, trapping six men. Two men were rescued after almost six days of being trapped; however, the remaining four men sadly lost their lives.

TODAY

Several remnants of mining and even railroad ruins are scattered throughout the wooded area. It is still apparent that this area was heavily mined. A portion of the ruins is said to be the base of the mining operations.

Above: One of the more complete ruins near Mocanaqua loop trail. This could have been a part of the coal mining operation.

Opposite above: It is apparent that some sort of structure was here. Most likely, a row of pillars to aid the coal mining carts.

Opposite below: A view from inside the more complete ruin near Mocanaqua loop trail. Notice the pit in the middle with debris.

On the other side of Mocanaqua loop trail appears to have been another structure. This could have been a building.

Nearby the more complete ruin, on top of a small cliff, rests a small building that could have been a part of the mining company.

Further down the trails are more building ruins.

Above right: A very large building ruin in the middle of the woods near Mocanaqua trail. Some say this could have been where the miners collected their pay.

A upper-level view from inside the very large building ruin.

Above left: It is not known whether this particular ruin was for the mining company or the railroad company.

Above right: This ruin served the railroad company.

5

ABANDONED ITALIAN WATER GARDEN

O nce a beautiful 32-acre estate owned by a loving couple, Oak Knoll was a mansion that had a very unique and attractive water garden area near Crum Creek. Lytlecote mansion was purchased by Ward and Edith Hickson in 1927, and later they renamed it Oak Knoll. The massive mansion was located above the water garden on a hillside where the highway, known as the Blue Route, is located now. It would have overlooked the immaculate water garden along with the creek that flows nearby.

Ward Hinkson had a passion for orchids and built a greenhouse near the mansion. Throughout their years together, they grew hundreds of orchids. Hinkson and his wife, Edith, began a business cultivating orchids for commercial sale, eventually adding more greenhouses, which resulted in the sale of over 100,000 orchids per year. Sadly, Edith passed away in 1957, but Ward continued to cultivate and sell orchids. Sales were usually the highest around Mother's Day.

In the early 1960s, the Hickson Family sold most of their 32-acre estate for residential construction. However, the construction of the Blue Route commenced, and the Oak Knoll mansion was in its path. The Hickson Family was forced to sell the remainder of their property, which included the Oak Knoll mansion, greenhouses and even the water garden.

By the early 1980s, Ward Hickson and his granddaughter watched with sorrow as the demolition of their beautiful property began, leveled to make way for the new superhighway.

Ward had built his life with his late wife on the very property that was being destroyed before his eyes. He passed away not too long after the demolition of his estate; perhaps he was heartbroken. His granddaughter recounted how depressing it was for them both.

The highway would eventually be completed in 1992.

TODAY

All that remains are the Italian Water Garden ruins with a stairway that once led to the beautiful mansion, in what is known now as Crum Woods just off the Leiper-Smedley Trail.

Where the water fountain pool was located is now just ground. It was filled in to avoid any accidents. Weeds grow throughout, but you can still find the bushes, trees and some flowers in the immediate area that were planted by the Hickson family.

It is difficult to tune out the sounds of vehicles that currently travel on the Blue Route since it's only yards away from the ruins.

This would have been the secondary main feature for the Italian water garden.

Stairways line the garden from both sides. In this picture, if you look in the distance you can see a white wall. The white wall is a sound barrier to the Blue Route.

From below the water garden looking up. This would have been an exit that leads to the creek.

6

BEAR VALLEY GHOST TOWN

Bear Valley used to be a mining village (also known as a mine patch) in the mid-1800s to the early 1900s. It had a one-room schoolhouse, a store, a few homes and a tunnel that went through the mountain. The one-mile tunnel is known as the Williamstown Tunnel and it was mined for anthracite coal. It was also used as a passageway for some of the workers that lived in Williamstown.

Located between Big Lick Mountain and the Bear Mountains, the mine patch of Bear Valley was founded to house the workers and their families of the Susquehanna Coal Company. The houses were built of simple materials and had no running water. The community had a water well that was the main water source until it dried up. Residents had to walk almost a mile to obtain water.

The area itself was dull—quite frankly, it was an eyesore. The village tried to spruce it up by adding colorful patches of gardens that had flowers, plants or vegetables.

The one-room schoolhouse was eventually split into four rooms to accommodate the number and ages of children that lived in the area. It is said growing up as a child in the Bear Valley was not terrible compared to other mining patches and villages at that time. There was a small swimming hole the children used to swim in. Recreation was created by the imagination of children. Sometimes the whole family would join in the fun.

TODAY

Few ruins still exist on what is now State Game Lands #264. There are absolutely no remnants of the structures that were made out of wood; however, several structures that were constructed out of concrete are still visible today. Some of the ruins are within a deer enclosure.

The Williamstown Tunnel is almost completely blocked off with fill, but you can see where the entrances are. It is not safe to explore in the tunnel as the spine is actively collapsing. There are deep mining pits, coal ash piles and other fragments from the coal mining industry found throughout the area.

Various types of thorn bearing trees and bushes encompassing the fields make this a difficult area to explore.

Above: One of a few ruins at Bear Valley Ghost Town. Notice how it is completely made of concrete. Most likely built in the early 1900s to 1920s.

The Williamstown Tunnel is almost completely blocked with fill. The spine is very weak and the tunnel is actively collapsing.

A part of the mining cart track.

Above left: Some of the ruins could not be reached due to the amount of thorn bushes in the area.

Above right: Another structure that we could not reach due to the thorn bushes.

A view of the field at Bear Valley Ghost Town. You can see the coal ash piles that look like large boulders out in a distance.

7

LAUSANNE GHOST TOWN

Some Pennsylvania ghost towns are well known, even to the locals that live near them. Lausanne (also known as Lausanne Landing) is one of those ghost towns and it turns out that even most of the locals are not aware of it. Lausanne is being reclaimed by nature deep in the woods of Pennsylvania state game lands. The only way to reach it is by hiking and crossing the river or stream, known as Jean's Run, that flows through the middle of the once-known town. It was not only built as a coal and railroad town in the early 1800s, but it was also known to build or repair boats to replace the damaged ones that crashed in the Lehigh River. The boats hauled coal down the Lehigh River and would repeatedly crash in the area, often losing their entire load of coal.

Carbon County's first post office was established here. It helped with the growth of the town. Lausanne also had a tavern and a sawmill that was likely water powered, fed from the dam nearby. The sawmill was located near the mouth of Nesquehoning River. The tavern also served as a toll gate, charging anyone a toll as they traveled through the town. This very well could have added to the demise of the town. People who traveled often avoided going through Lausanne to avoid paying the toll.

Josiah White was the owner of Lehigh Coal and Navigation Company and he had his sights on purchasing Lausanne, drawing up plans for residential growth of the town. Unfortunately, the town was plagued with floods and the property price was set too high for any buyer that had an interest in purchasing the land. With the growth of other coal and railroad towns booming nearby, Lausanne didn't stand a chance, with flooding being the biggest issue. In the 1830s, the town was placed up for public sale after Josiah White was unsuccessful in obtaining the land. Eventually, Lausanne was left to decay. No one else expressed interest in purchasing the land.

TODAY

There are a few structures still standing; one is more complete than the others. It is not known what these structures could have been used for. They could have been homes or simply storage areas, but one thing for sure is the two stone structures by Jean's Run was a bridge. It is elevated and you can visually imagine it being connected over Jean's Run at one point.

The main trail that runs through the town could have been the beginning of the Lehigh and Susquehenna turnpike that Josiah White had envisioned, but it never came into full fruition.

A portion of the area is an active archaeological dig, recovering artifacts from the American Indians that once lived in this forest. It is a protected area.

Above: A trail surrounded by rhododendrons that leads to the pipe bridge in Lausanne.

Below: The pipe bridge. Can be very dangerous to cross.

One of the more complete ruins at Lausanne. Notice that there are no areas for windows.

Stones protrude out of the side of the building. This could have been used to climb to the roof.

Above left: More ruins are scattered throughout this area.

Above right: Some call this Stagecoach Road, but this most likely could have been the start of the Susquehenna turnpike that Josiah White had envisioned. This leads around the mountain.

Above right: Jean's Run stream runs through Lausanne.

The half of the bridge that once ran across Jean's Run.

The second half of the bridge.

8

THOMAS IRON MILLS RUINS

A Welsh ironmaster immigrant by the name of David Thomas built a coal powered hot blast iron furnace in the 1840s in the Lehigh Valley area. Due to his success and impressive knowledge of ironmaking, he expanded his operations throughout the region. Thomas was also known as the "Father of the American anthracite iron industry."

The main plant was erected in Hokendauqua and his company continued expansion in the area, including the town of Coplay. In 1862, in addition to the furnaces and plants, Thomas purchased a one-and-a-half-mile railroad line that would support his company.

Owning four mines and joint ownership of a fifth in 1875, Thomas's company produced massive quantities of iron, affirming his abilities with ironmaking. The expansion of operations included more iron furnaces, and having a railroad system near the area made the operation of hauling ore and iron much more manageable over the traditional horse and wagon. Thomas's family continued to expand and acquired more mines, furnaces and other iron companies.

By the early 1900s, the iron industry began to decline. Anthracite coal was mostly replaced with coke and foreign ores, abolishing any competitive edge Thomas's Iron Company had retained. By 1921, the company was in such decline that it could not recover. Eventually, in 1922, the company sold its stock to Drexel & Company and they liquidated assets.

TODAY

Many of the Thomas Iron Works ruins can be seen throughout the Hokendauqua and Coplay area. Some are preserved and others are being reclaimed by nature.

The Ironton Railtrail spans nine miles in Lehigh County and most of the ruins are along this public trial.

Further southeast of the trail near the Lehigh River, which is said to be private land, lie a few of the ruins that are being reclaimed, including the large old engine house ruin that repaired locomotives, an abandoned train trestle with rail line and other buildings. There is also a tunnel that is said to have housed water and gas mains.

Right: These large ruins were once a locomotive repair building, where locomotives were pulled inside to be repaired.

Below: A view from inside the locomotive repair building.

Above left: Concrete ruins near the river that was a part of Thomas Iron Works.

Above left: One of three corridors inside the concrete ruin near the river.

Above right: This tunnel could have been used to house water and gas mains.

Abandoned train bridge near the main trail.

Abandoned train trestle that goes over the main trail.

Note the layers of stone and how nature finds ways to reclaim.

9

POQUESSING CREEK RUINS

Along the Poquessing Creek near Bensalem are the sizable ruins of a former bank barn built in the late 1700s, which was owned by the Townsend family. The property was eventually sold to the City of Philadelphia in 1831 after Evan Townsend passed away. The city converted the bank barn to a prison farm building to put prisoners to work. They grew crops mainly to feed other fellow prisoners. In addition to the large bank barn ruin, there were also two greenhouses along with a pump house and an office. In 1968, the prison farm had permanently closed. The structures remained mostly intact until the early 1970s.

TODAY

The large bank barn ruins can be seen from the Poquessing Creek Trail in Philadelphia County near Bensalem, but it is deteriorating. It was originally a stone structure later reinforced with concrete that is still apparent today. A few walls have collapsed, but other walls and the loading dock still remain.

The layout of the smaller ruin that still exists indicate that it could have been a pump house. It is near where the greenhouses were once located.

This was a bank barn turned into a building for the prison farm. You can see what appears to be a loading dock on the right side. Stonework is apparent under the concrete it was once lined with.

Above left: This hole could have been for drainage.

10

RIDLEY CREEK
STATE PARK RUINS

O riginally known as Providence Mills until 1785 and later Bishop Mills until 1862, a village was built around what is now known as Sycamore Mills. Farmsteads also populated the area.

Initially built as a water corn mill in the early 1700s, Bishop Mills was later converted and produced a variety of metal materials. Operating until 1828, it had an adjoining sawmill. The ownership of the mill exchanged hands a number of times until 1901 when it was destroyed by a fire. Most of the property was purchased by the State of Pennsylvania in 1960. By 1976, the park was registered as a Historic District with the National Register of Historic Places.

TODAY

There are several ruins scattered throughout Ridley Creek State Park. Most of what remains were once homes, barns and spring houses. Unprotected from the elements and visitors, some are in surprisingly good condition considering how old they are. They date to the late 1600s to the early 1900s. Made of mostly stone and brick, they have withstood the strong storms nature has thrown at them so far, but are still considered fragile. Roofs can even still be found on a few of them, but caution is advised if you choose to explore, as they are on the verge of collapse. A few of the original homesteads were converted for modern use, which today are being utilized as homes.

A view of inside of what is said to be the Mosser house.

A view of the outside of the Mosser house.

Above left: This is a smaller ruin along one of the upper trails. This could have been a spring house.

A chimney stands alone on top of the hill near one of the parking areas. No other remnants are around this chimney.

11

ROLLING HILL PARK RUINS

Within the 103 acres of the park known as Rolling Hill in Gladwyne are quite a few ruins that have their own story.

Barker Mill is the last surviving mill out of more than twenty various types of mills that once existed in the area. Built in the late 1700s, the mill originally manufactured military weapons and gunpowder. The ownership of the property changed at some point in the early 1800s and the Nippes family were the new owners of the mill. They produced guns and rifles that were supplied for the U.S. during the War of 1812. Later, it was purchased by William Booth around 1886 and he converted the mill to produce carpet yarn.

The present name of the mill derived from Thomas Baker, who eventually purchased the mill in 1923 and produced spun wool up until the 1950s. In the 1970s, the mill was converted to conform to more modern businesses.

The three stone ruins, close in proximity to the mill that was built in the mid-1800s, once housed mill workers. They were multi-dwelling structures that accommodated not only the mill workers, but their families as well. This was a way for the mill owners to ensure that their employees worked their hardest. But the reality was that the owners utilized it to control their workers, giving them only minimal amounts of time to eat, rest and spend time with their families.

Closer to the mill, there is another housing-type stone structure. This could have been a single-family dwelling, perhaps for the mill foreman.

There are a few ruins near the parking area that were once a farm. In its heyday, the farm had a barn, cottage and a stable. The area wasn't known for its agricultural farming, but it was sold as such. It was named Folly Farm when Irwin Megargee realized he had made a mistake in purchasing the land that was not primed for crop. When Irwin Megargee passed away, his wife sold the property to Paul C.

Hagenlocher. During this time, building structures with concrete was the "new age" of building. He added concrete structures to the property, which still exist today, including the concrete silo.

TODAY

Some remnants of the farm, tenements and stone houses still exist today, but are not fully intact. The mill is fully intact, but modernized, and it is privately owned.

There are a few trails in the park and a few of them will lead you to the ruins. A short walk from the parking lot are the farming ruins. The tenements for the mill workers are located downhill near the creek, about a one-and-a-half-mile hike from the parking lot.

Above: Nature is clearly winning with this ruin.

Below: An old retaining wall near the farm ruins.

The farm ruins. Note the concrete silo in the background still stands.

Some ruins are more visible during the winter; this is one of them. Weeds cover these ruins during spring and summer.

Above left: A tenement house for the mill workers. This was the larger of the three.

The second tenement house.

The third tenement house. A sign in front indicates that the ruins are protected.

Above left: The converted Baker Mill as it stands today. When we visited, it was for sale.

Above right: One of the farm ruins near the parking lot.

There is a ruin under all those vines.

12

MONOCACY HILL QUARRY RUINS

The John T. Dyer Quarry Company purchased land in the 1920s for his quarry operation and built a large structure in 1925. However, the stone crushing building never saw a day of operation, because the crucial railroad system that was supposed to be in place never happened. Eager to get the quarry operation started, John T. Dyer Company had most of the equipment shipped and already on site even before the railroad was built. The railroad was a crucial part of the operation. The quarry crusher was built to have railroad cars pulled underneath it for loading.

When local residents heard the announcement about the quarry company's intentions to excavate the mountain at that time, removing very large quantities of trap rock, they protested in great numbers. It is not known if the protesting of local residents or the failure of the railroad system (or a combination of both) led to the abandonment of the operation.

Finally, in 1967, Amity Township purchased the 400+ acres of Monocacy Hill, which included the ruins, for recreation and open space purposes.

TODAY

The ruins can be found on one of the lower trails. There are a few ruins here, including the remains of the lower half of the stone crusher building.

The quarry crusher. The lower portion is all that remains. This lower portion would have served the railroad cars as they would have been pulled underneath to be loaded.

I am assuming this would have been a part of either the quarry operations or a part of the railroad system that was never completed—or both.

13

DELHAAS WOODS RUINS

Nature has started to reclaim ruins in DelHaas Woods that once were ammunition storage buildings during World War II. Leaves falling and naturally composting throughout the years have created the perfect growing environment for small trees and bushes on top of the ruins.

There were once three large warehouse-sized buildings in this area, but the third building was demolished by 1958. Other smaller buildings were once in the area as well. They had large dirt mounds built around them in case of an explosion. All that remains of those smaller buildings today are large dirt mounds. After the war ended, the remaining two buildings were repurposed to serve regular businesses.

TODAY

The ruins are a part of the Silver Lake Nature Center 468 acres park property. All that remains are the foundations of these buildings, but one building still has a wall, which unfortunately attracts vandalism.

The dirt horseshoe shaped mounds can be found throughout Delhaas Woods. These would have surrounded buildings that contained explosives.

Peering through the large gaping hole, you can see what the underneath of the warehouse-sized foundation looks like. It is only about 4 feet in height, but it runs the length of the foundation.

Giving a perspective on how long the foundations are, I had two people stand on the opposite side. They are hard to see because they are that far away.

Above: The second foundation still has a wall intact. It is the epicenter for graffiti.

Left: A telephone pole remains.

14

MARSH CREEK RUINS

Once a community built of mills and farms, Marsh Creek State Park was formerly known as Millford Mills. It played an important role in creating goods and growing crops for Chester County until the much-needed water management plan was put in place and a dam was built to help create the lake.

Millford Mills had its own small schoolhouse, mills, general store, covered bridge and a few homes and barns. The community dates to the late 1800s. Unfortunately, the area was prone to floods and droughts—there was no in-between. A water management plan had to be put in place, not only for the immediate surrounding communities, but for the surrounding counties as well. Acquisition of the properties in the area began by the State of Pennsylvania in 1968 and the process continued until all the properties were purchased. Some property owners were resistant, understandably reluctant to leave the homes they knew. The resistance from the owners lasted two years, trying everything they could to save their property, but ultimately the State won.

Construction of the dam began in the early 1970s. Later clearing out brush, trees and debris, a valley was formed where the lake was to be created. The dam to Marsh Creek was completed and by 1974, Marsh Creek Reservoir was in place. It took three years for the creek to fill the lake to the right level.

TODAY

While most of the structures were taken down, some foundations were left behind. A few are under the lake to this day. Other remnants are scattered throughout the park, including the stairs that once led to a mansion.

Stairs that once led to the mansion.

Above left: In terms of seeing ruins, a quadruple serving fireplace is a rare sight. The lower portions would have been in the sectioned basement, while the upper portion would have served divided rooms.

Above right: This ruin is collapsing in on itself.

Above right: A drainage pipe near the mansion

Wood support beams can still be seen.

15

WISSAHICKON VALLEY RUINS

A few ruins can be found in Wissahickon Valley Park, Some served more mysterious purposes than others.

The wide, partially paved trail now known as Forbidden Drive was originally named Wissahickon Drive. It was built in the mid-1850s with mills all along the drive near dams that helped power them. Some of the dams can still be seen today, but very small remnants of the mills remain, as only a few stone walls against the riverbanks.

Along Forbidden Drive are ruins of what appears to be a guard station. Embedded into the hillside, this stone structure is unique. Peering inside of it is almost like peering into a jail cell flooded with discolored water. A decorative stone wall is in front of this ruin, making it a picturesque beauty that is gracefully aging along Forbidden Drive.

Further up the trail, the mountain was once tapped for drinking water that served the travelers along the turnpike in 1854. It looked like it could have been a concrete doorway into the mountain. The inscription on the large plaque of the fountain reads, "Pro Bono Publico, Esta Perpetua" which translates into "For the good of the public, let it remain forever."

The mysterious Cave of Kelpius is also within Wissahickon Valley Park. It is believed that the cave was created by cult leader, mystic Johannes Kelpius, in 1694. Kelpius and his followers believed that the world was going to end and sought the solitude in nature the valley offered only to wait for the end of days. They passed time meditating and being one with nature. Kelpius passed away in 1708. Much of his group of followers remained in the area and assimilated back to society, taking on occupations.

TODAY

The Cave of Kelpius remains, but has been gutted due to vandalism. It is a very small cave lined with stone. The entrance is built into the hillside with a stone plaque detailing its history. The "guard station" is still fully intact. You cannot enter as the gate is closed and locked, but you can walk up and view the small room inside. Both the fountain and the "guard station" are located along Forbidden Drive.

The assumed guard station.

Opposite above: It's not very big inside and water is collecting.

Opposite below: The unique design of the stone wall. It either had a water feature or a water trough for horses.

Above: Retaining wall for a mill that was nearby.

Below left: All that remains of a mill towards the left side. This was across the river.

Below right: The public drinking fountain.

Kelpius cave.

A look inside Kelpius cave. Stone is lining the inside.

16

ABANDONED AND IN RUIN

While these locations are not exactly abandoned ruins, they are certainly abandoned and in ruin.

Turn Hole Tunnel

A 496-foot railroad tunnel is now an abandoned tunnel near Jim Thorpe, Pennsylvania. It once had two tracks built by the Lehigh and Susquehanna Railroad Company, and was leased to Central Railroad of New Jersey.

The name "Turn Hole" was derived from the deep eddy in the river that the tunnel is next to. An eddy is where the water flow of the river swirls in one place, usually because of an obstruction. In this case, the obstruction is Moyer's Rocks.

The tunnel was bored in 1866 and mainly used by the Central Railroad of New Jersey's main line until 1910, when it was condemned. The railroad initiated plans to construct a bypass in 1911 and it was completed by 1912. The two tracks in the tunnel were continued to be used as a passing siding until 1956. Shortly after, the tunnel and its tracks were abandoned.

Today

The tunnel has minor collapses. Railroad ties for both tracks can still be found, but they are not in alignment. If you look close enough in the areas along the outside of the portal entrance near the parking lot, you can spot a few feet of the railroad tracks.

The pillars that were once a part of the railroad bridge coming out of the north portal are still standing in Lehigh River.

The portal near the parking lot.

Both tracks can still be seen

Looking out the north portal. This side comes out over the river.

Railroad track by the portal near the parking lot.

CENTRALIA

Centralia was once a bustling town that had plenty of homes and shops. It was a coal mining community with a number of Molly Macquires members. The town of Centralia met its fate in 1962, when a fire was started by the town's garbage dump near one of the abandoned mines.

There are several theories circulating as to how the fire started. One of those theories states that it was a town official that had deliberately started the fire in celebration of Memorial Day in 1962 to have the dump cleaned up; another is that a cigarette was thrown from one of the trash workers and set the trash pile on fire. Regardless, the fire reached the coal veins in the mine and burned underground for decades.

It wasn't until 1969 that the residents started noticing the effects of the mine fire burning below. People started to get sick from the smoke and ash. Measures were taken to try to put the fire out, but all were in vain.

In 1992, the government stepped up and bought the residents out, stripping Centralia of its zip code. Only a few residents decided to stay.

TODAY

Not much remains today—only a couple homes along with the abandoned portion Route 61 (also known as Graffiti Highway). A few remnants can be found outside of Graffiti Highway, but most abandoned houses and other buildings have been torn down.

An old railroad track bed can be found not far from Graffiti Highway, but no rail ties or tracks can be seen.

Above left: Route 61, also known as Graffiti Highway.

Above right: One of the venting pipes.

A coal machine remains.

This building could have been a garage or a shed.

BIBLIOGRAPHY

BOOKS

Martindale, Joseph C. *A History of the Township of Byberry and Moreland in Philadelphia, PA,* 1867

Poliniak, Louis. *When Coal Was King,* 1970

ARTICLES

"Report Spread That West End Coal Co. Will Quit." *The Mountain Echo,* 11 Mar. 1938, https://www.newspapers.com/clip/9499305/jed_irish_west_end_coal_company

Thompson, Patty. "Rolling Hill Park, Lower Merion's Big Treasure." *Main Line Times,* 3, Oct. 2013, www.mainlinemedianews.com/mainlinetimes/opinion/patty-thompson-rolling-hill-park-lower-merion-s-big-treasure/article_41541ffc-2ec6-5b47-b645-2ebefb60ea51

"Will Likely Save Monocacy Hill From Destruction." *Reading Eagle,* 21 Feb. 1925, www.news.google.com/newspapers?nid=1955&dat=19250220&id=F6YhAAAAI-BAJ&sjid=R5oFAAAAIBAJ&pg=4156,3985897&hl=en

WEBSITES

www.alhs18011.org/lock-ridge-furnace-history--preservation.html

www.archive.org/stream/preservationinri00barr#page/n3/mode/1up

www.centraliapa.org/history-centralia-pa-1962-1977

www.chroniclingamerica.loc.gov, The Fulton County news, June 01, 1904, Image 2

www.coalmininghistorypa.org

www.dcnr.pa.gov/StateParks/FindAPark/RidleyCreekStatePark/Pages/History.aspx

www.delawarecountyhistory.com/edgmonttownship/documents/TheSycamoreMill.pdf

www.earthconservancy.org

www.explorepahistory.com

www.exploringnjandpa.com

www.fow.org/visit-the-park/structures-landmarks

www.himedo.net/TheHopkinThomasProject/CoalFireIronSteel/Appendices/
  CatasauquaIndustryResidences/DaleWint_TheIronBorough.htm#ThomasIron

www.history.com/news/mine-fire-burning-more-50-years-ghost-town

www.lowermerionhistory.org/texts/first300/part31.html, Rolling Hill Park

www.mcall.com, Thomas Iron burned bright for 88 years

www.monroehistorical.org

www.nextooze.com/explore-the-thomas-iron-works-ruins/

www.poconoheritage.blogspot.com

www.scottarboretum.org

www.sepahiking.blogspot.com, Monocacy Hill Recreation Area

www.sites.google.com/site/marshcreekstateparkhistory/history

www.slicesofamerica.com/wissahickon-valley-park

www.stuofdoom.com

www.swarthmorephoenix.com

www.treasurenet.com, Bear Valley Ghost Town, Dauphin County

www.usminedisasters.miningquiz.com

www.vfmountain.org

www.waymarking.com/waymarks/WMC5EM_Turn_Hole_Glen_Onoko_Tunnel

Misc.

Northeast Philadelphia History Network, *Facebook Message*, "Re: I'm looking for some information on the ruins near the Poquessing Creek trail that is near the Bensalem border..." Received by Kathleen Butler, 19 June 2019

Online Video

The Wandering Woodsman. (2018, Jan. 18). *Tunnels and Old Trucks in the Ghost Town of Bear Valley*. www.youtube.com/watch?v=zIcfVgzhL9A